First Bite

...where it all began

mindful mouthfuls • simple savouring • tuned-in tasting • blissful bites

FIRST BITE

First Bite
by David Jones and Pamela Bray

Book design Pamela Bray

© 2023 All rights reserved
ISBN 978-0-6450110-2-9

Contents

The beginning   1

Onions, clarity, resolution (about this book)   2

The first meal   5

Ninth bite   6

Grey or colour?   8

Three's company, four's a crowd   9

TRY IT Place cards   12

TRY IT Grace   13

First *real* curry   14

THE SCIENCE Like a virgin   17

TRY IT The luxurious slow   18

My big stop   19

Chow down   20

THE SCIENCE Saliva   23

Ron's napkin   25

Morning tea   27

THE SCIENCE Peeling back the onion   28

TRY IT Three mindful breaths   29

Ma's madeira   31

TRY IT Origins   34

TRY IT Guided gratitude meditation   36

TRY IT Partner meditation   38

TRY IT More place cards   40

TRY IT Drink coasters   42

Next steps... over to you   43

The beginning

A few years back, we travelled to Bali. Workshops called "Search Inside Yourself"* were being held around the globe and Bali was closest to our home in Sydney. These two-day workshops had been spun out of Google to enable workplace mindfulness experiences, based on neuroscience. Curious to try it out for ourselves and having practised meditation for three decades, we wanted to know what the latest in science could teach us.

How to describe the two days? Extremely full, surprisingly beneficial and sweatingly tropical. Amongst strangers, hearing the familiar expressed with different words, and the intensity of each long day, it certainly reminded us of how much more we can be, every single day.

While the workshops didn't tell us much that was new, one practical exercise had a profound effect and stayed with us, enough to spark the idea for this book. It was the exercise of bringing awareness to the first three bites in each meal.

Sounds simple, right? But like most things that appear easy, the practical reality is anything but. It sent us on an exploration of how to make this an everyday practice – a mindful "First Bite".

Our holidays mostly take the form of exploring, adventures and trekking, but occasionally short, lying around, relaxing holidays *do* happen. The few days after the course was one such time. Doing nothing by the pool is not our thing so, after the workshop concluded, writing was our go-to.

Over those four or so days, the themes for this book were born and most of it written. Four to five hours of writing each day, then the often emotional exercise of reading our offerings to each other.

Wind forward a couple of years and many meals. Fresh eyes gave the book this structure:
- where the idea for the book came from
- simple daily exercises you can try (**TRY IT**)
- tales of real-life people (Story)
- some science for the nerds (THE SCIENCE).

We hope what follows in this book can be a reminder for you to also slow down, savour your food, your friends and your life.

* Search Inside Yourself Leadership Institute (SIYLI - and yes, pronounced "silly") siyli.org

Onions, clarity, resolution

ABOUT THIS BOOK

Onions have layers, so too does human experience. But our minds have a way of turning nuance into absolutes, giving a unique moment a label and putting this in a box.

But, as the saying goes, "the map is not the territory" – the moment we label an experience we make a map and lose real clarity on that experience. We perceive the onion as only the outer layer and miss experiencing the sweeter inner layers.

First Bite is about going as deep into the onion as you wish. "Eating mindfully" can be yet another throw-away label – a quip, a one-line scold, an intellectual construct, a T-shirt slogan – and that's okay.

But this book's purpose is to set the bar way, way lower (and higher at the same time). We learned that if you get to First Bite, then Second Bite is **now** possible for you. Second Bite is really just another First Bite.

Why does this matter?

We believe eating is the second most natural and spirit-enhancing act any living being can perform. Eating is a profound transformation of food into energy, sensation and by-products.

First Bite is so bloody simple that it's nothing more than the tiniest shift in your eating. When practising First Bite, you may experience flavours, textures, attention, reduced distraction and an awareness of how mindlessly we normally consume our food.

During the book we offer some fruits of mindful eating. The idea is that this micro-practice will deliver changes for you, your interactions with others, and lead to other benefits such as calmness, **aliveness** and better digestion.

Call to action

In a podcast, the neuroscientist, author and prominent atheist Sam Harris summarised the societal changes around mindfulness: "Only a few decades ago doctors were smoking in their treatment rooms and appeared in advertisements for cigarettes. Today they would lose their right to treat patients. So too mindfulness is transitioning from beads and baggy pants to mainstream, supported by the weight of scientific evidence that makes it a no-brainer in personal well-being."

From a societal perspective, reduced reactivity – one positive outcome of mindfulness – can reduce violent responses, prevent everyday ills, such as road-rage through to helping those in distress, to such a degree that it's taught to sufferers of PTSD, positioned not as a panacea but a viable therapeutic tool.

First Bite is a simple call-to-action, to start each and every meal with three mindful bites, and observe the contribution to your life and others around you.

Oh, by the way, the "first" natural and spirit-enhancing act is "First Breath". Many wisdom traditions start with an awareness of breath.

First meal

Eighty minutes after we had been given "mindfully take the first three bites of your meal" as a homework assignment, we were sitting in one of the hundreds of small eateries in Ubud's town centre.

My seventh or eighth mouthful of basil beef had been chewed and swallowed before I remembered. Pam's chicken pica pica was also well underway.

"I forgot to mindfully take my first three bites," I said with more than a shade of shame. My eyes rested on Pam and she blinked back at me as if her hands had been caught in the till. She sheepishly replied, "Me too."

We had both forgotten.

It wasn't as though we were rushed or arguing or trying to remind ourselves of some long-forgotten ancient practice – it was a mere 80 minutes since the task had been given!

Of course we had **NOT** forgotten.

The SIYLI people would suggest our meta-awareness did actually bring it back to our conscious awareness, just a little late and so we were *actually* being **good** practitioners.

We laughed. The workshop was already paying dividends – we had been sceptical but had already learned a valuable lesson.

As an Australian having spent significant time in Silicon Valley, when a Californian says "mindfulness", the hairs on my neck stand up. But when you've paid travel, accommodation and conference fees, it's much easier to let go of that petty objection – I am "all-in".

We wanted to see how Google packaged meditation for its hard-nosed rationalist world of engineers, and how a group who might traditionally think of meditation as "woo" could literally be wooed to new practices that they could use at work.

Some scepticism still remained – perhaps Google just wanted us all to be better corporate drones.

Ninth bite

Our Ninth Bite was joyfully shared, tinged with a little leftover guilt. It was quiet, still, and more alive than any of the bites I'd taken that week. When you've been a couple for 30-something years, life can become habitual, the jobs of everyday life getting knocked over on autopilot.

The preparation and consumption of meals is one of those rhythms that becomes incredibly transactional: you lock in a decision on what it is, execute the preparation and consume with the efficiency of a well-programmed droid.

This Ninth Bite was rich. It was intimate, as we shared the food – together. It didn't matter that we were eating different things, feeling different textures, chewing at slightly different rates, tasting different ingredients and sitting across from each other facing different backdrops.

Sharing a simple lovely intimacy stretched out between us.

Meanwhile, the movement-addicted monkey mind is screaming to "get on with it". Small sentences forced their way into my mind: "this is stupid", "it's taking too long", "enough is enough", "you'll be here until midnight at this rate", "TWO BITES TO GO".

But, remember, the exercise given from SIYLI wasn't First Bite. It was *first three bites*! The mounting pressure internally to abandon the exercise was approaching nuclear fusion (or is it fission – I can never remember) characteristics but luckily years of present-moment-awareness practice also had a place at the table.

In the internal conversation, the words "Let it go" felt like a silent whisper softening each moment. I could almost hear some harem-pants-wearing 30-something girl barely exhaling the words at the shavasana end of a yoga session. "Let it gooo…"

Miraculously, I took her advice. I could suddenly taste the sweetness of the basil, the crunch of the lightly fried carrot alongside the warm density of the beef – time stretched out. I could feel more space now.

This experience was a subtle yet powerful shift and really encapsulates the purpose of this book.

And so, the tenth and eleventh bites were taken and shared with some ongoing monkey-mind histrionics but perhaps with a little less agitation. The negotiation was simply that "you get the rest of the meal if you just share the first three bites". Done deal.

From the twelfth bite we allowed ourselves to just throttle back and luxuriate in the meal. It wasn't some cosmic experience, nor was it some reductive dry assessment. We simply enjoyed *bon temps*, textures, tastes and crunch – a full body experience.

Grey or Colour?

Have you seen a movie where the star-struck lover's world turns from grey to colour?

*In that moment they see **more**, have more gratitude, have more spontaneity, more **presence**, and they seem more joyous.*

*Practising First Bite **turns on the colour** – at least on your taste buds. The very first bite of food has a much stronger taste and creates a stronger sensation than all that follow. In contrast, when our mind is elsewhere and lost in thought – "I really need to get on with [insert your current urgency]" each bite is more and more ordinary, resetting us from colour back to grey.*

*Returning again and again to First Bite builds **muscle** in the tug-of-war between "grey" and living colour. Treat each bite like the first bite for as long as you can. With gentle persistence you may also find you grow your gratitude, observational richness, even **presence** :)*

*Think of someone you know who lives with more **presence** and observable **aliveness**. By developing **muscle** with First Bite, **you** could be that example.*

First Bite – It's small and simple but, at the same time, big and complex. Every conscious decision you make about your food makes a difference to you and possibly those around you!

Don't underestimate your power.

Three's company, four's a crowd

They say Melbourne has four seasons in one day, so too Ubud has a cycle that repeats each day.

By lunchtime, the second season was well underway. The blue expanse of sky resigns itself to compete with the fluff-balls of cumulonimbus. The tropical sun seeps into your skin, occasionally bracketed by the clouds, so an oscillation of intense bursts of heat and moments of shaded relief plays over your body. But the cumulative effect results in an urge, just below the surface of your consciousness, that is nagging you for just a waft of cool breeze to show up.

So, too, with the verdant landscape. The moisture from last night's shower and the dew of the morning surrenders to steam under the escalating heat. The turbulence of the river below the resort restaurant, where the workshop is being held, adds to the overall thickness of the air. My skin doesn't quite have a sheen but there is enough moistness for my clothing to stick uncomfortably to my skin. Today is particularly intense and, when you are not accustomed to the heat, it wears you down and an unspoken testiness lurks within and hovers like a shadow.

It's lunch break. David and I have been seated a little while with Isabella, another participant in the workshop. Our initial tentative conversation quickly found an easy rhythm, talking about the day, our work and what passions underlay it. The food had just arrived and gently taunted me with its creative presentation and total yummyness, whilst the conversation eased along.

It won't surprise you that the workshop had again given us the lunchtime exercise of three mindful bites and with the tautness akin to being on a first date, our threesome silently formed a contract to undertake the exercise together.

It's awkward doing something outside the norm with strangers. "Will I look pretentious?" "How should I look anyway?" "Can I be mindful and fast?" "What happens if I finish first, should I

speak?" blah, blah, blah, blah, blaaaah – monkey mind is a super valuable companion in times like this – NOT.

So amongst words of "shall we?" and a resigned sigh of "three mindful bites", we began to serve the morsels from the bamboo and palm-leaved platters onto our plates. Our fourth member arrived (the square tables were set for four), and with only a few words spoken, my cringe rose up in me – yes, she was Australian.

I allow my judgemental nature to subside and let Number Four just be Number Four. A few brief welcomes and I figure the best way to deal with the discomfort, that at least I was feeling, was to announce, "We are just starting our three mindful bites".

Being given the exercise only five minutes earlier, I had a reasonable expectation that "Great – I'm ready" would be a socially appropriate response.

Instead Number Four shot out, "Ahh, I'm not good at that stuff" and continued on with a very long sentence about something. My impassioned glance at Isabelle and David, hoping to be rescued, was left unanswered. They had suddenly become very mindful of their plates! I followed their lead as a way of escape, looking intently at my fork as I scooped up the first morsel. I felt our contract (the three of us) had taken a blow to the bow, but our ship wasn't sunk yet.

We each took our silent mouthfuls while nodding at the ongoing stream of verbal something or others from Number Four. We limped through our three bites and the whole experience was a rich lesson of what *making change* in the world is like. There will always be challenges and resistance to making a new way, but there is still wiggle room when the work is small, personal, intimate and fortified by an intention.

This is not a criticism of Number Four. We've all been Number Four, and we all will be Number Four again, over and over.

By the way, Number Four wanted to become a SIYLI coach – I hope they do it authentically, and any student sees this by their actions, not because they hold a paper certificate.

TRY IT

Grace

Regardless of whether you are secular or Christian or Jedi (!), the practice of saying grace is a wonderful way to create a stop prior to chowing down.

Your grace may be just three deep breaths.

Your grace may be something simple, spoken aloud or silently worded.
It might be:

We are grateful for:
the food we are about to eat,
for the friends that share this food and
the earth, air, water and people that nurtured it.

Or:

"We are grateful to allow this food to complete its purpose
and that it may be consciously used by us to pay those gifts forward in our deeds".

If these seem forced, then simple appreciation shared with the chef is equally good.

The classic Australian 1990s movie *The Castle* shows how it's done properly:
Darrel: *What do you call this luv?*
Sal: *Ice cream.*
Darrel: *But yeah, it's what you do with it.*
Dale: *How do you do it Mum?*
Sal: *Scooped it out of the punnet.*

First real curry

I grew up in a meat and three veg household, and I didn't eat meat! My mother also had the not-incorrect notion that everyone should sit down to dinner at the same time. So meal preparations were done, vegetables chopped (quite a lot of raw vegies were consumed by me straight off the chopping board), peas shelled (again as many went into my mouth as into the bowl).

Food was put on the stove, and there it stayed until everyone was at the table. Needless to say this mostly ended up as a plate of meat and mushy vegetables – never my fave. I always preferred them raw. And having snacked during their preparation, I was never hungry by the time we sat down.

Dinner was arduous – cutting off small pieces of meat, pushing them around my plate, hiding them under the mushy peas. When forced to put some in my mouth I would chew once, move it around my mouth and ultimately get it back to the plate in a way, I thought at the time, no-one would notice. I just couldn't swallow it. Even as a toddler, I didn't like the smell, taste or texture. Many times, when everyone had finished and left the table, I would still be sitting there, my mother having rewarmed my meal over a saucepan of boiling water, urging me to eat some more. It was a trial for me and for her, poor thing.

Relief came occasionally when we would get fish and chips from the local, usually on a Friday night, wrapped in newspaper. And very, very occasionally there was a visit to the local Chinese restaurant for curried prawns and rice – with its mild yellow creamy sauce. In my childhood household food was a simple affair, spaghetti came with tomato sauce in a tin and avocados didn't exist.

My late teens was a time when the wider world suddenly revealed itself in a flurry of independence that came with a curiosity and passion to discover everything (having friends with cars helped). Through a group of close friends, new music found me, art and architecture became a passion, questions about the universe were suddenly on my lips and food, too, emerged as an exciting new experience. Spaghetti came without red sauce! Olive oil, garlic, herbs and an *al dente* texture transformed it from a snack on soggy toast to an exotic flavour sensation.

One particularly memorable Saturday night, our group ventured to a renowned curry place in North Sydney. This was not my backyard. New impressions ignited me, synapses firing with new experiences. Most of my friends were more "worldly" than me – or so I believed at the time – so food was ordered from their recommendations. No meat for me!

As the food started to arrive, I remember being surprised by the arrangement of dishes placed on the table. This was no "one plate per person" place. Everything was in small copper bowls and placed in the centre of the table. There were curries of different colours, banana with coconut on top (!?) (we didn't WTF in those days 😊), yoghurt and mint, and a large basket filled with huge crispy papadums. This was all so new.

Taking my friend's lead, I helped myself to rice and some bright orange vegetable curry. It was powerfully aromatic with spices I wasn't sure I'd ever smelled before. Loading up my fork, lifting it to my mouth, the intensity of the aroma rising, and then that first mouthful. Nothing could have prepared me for the intensity of the flavour. But then the heat hit me. My mouth was on fire, my lips numbing by the second. I grabbed the water and downed the whole glass. Not helping.

"Here, this is better than water," Muzz said, only smiling slightly, as he handed me the banana and coconut. Slightly better. By now everyone was laughing. "Good, isn't it? Best in Sydney." My second bite had more rice, less curry. I needn't have worried – my mouth was still on fire and I couldn't taste a thing. But the cooling accompaniments stayed at my end of the table.

That night a door opened for me. Curry was not just a mild creamy yellow sauce with prawns. As with many things at that time, I was a few bites more worldly wise, even if I was short a few taste buds.

THE SCIENCE

Like a virgin
The science of "first time".

Just like your first real curry, any first experience is often powerfully remembered due to a psychological phenomenon called the novelty effect. When we encounter something new, our brains are wired to pay more attention to the novel stimulus as a survival mechanism to identify potential threats or opportunities.

This heightened attention leads to increased activity in the hippocampus, a region of the brain responsible for memory formation, as well as the release of dopamine (yeeehaaaa!), which plays a role in motivation, reward, and memory consolidation.

So, the first experience of something is encoded more strongly in our memory, making it more vivid and easier to recall later on.

Making each meal memorable

Give your hippocampus a daily workout. Being mindful and present when eating focuses your attention on "now", being aware of your thoughts, feelings and surroundings without judgment.

This heightened awareness leads to better encoding and consolidation of memories, as you are more fully engaged in the experience.

When you are mindful and present, you pay attention to details and fully immerse yourself in the eating (or whatever you are doing). This focused attention allows you to form richer, more vivid memories by enhancing the encoding process, which is the initial stage of forming a memory. Every time builds **muscle**.

There is some evidence that mindfulness practices can help improve cognitive function, increase cerebral blood flow, and protect against age-related cognitive decline.

And just a richer life!

Chiesa, A., Calati, R., & Serretti, A. (2011). Does mindfulness training improve cognitive abilities? A systematic review of neuropsychological findings. Clinical Psychology Review, 31(3), 449-464.
https://doi.org/10.1016/j.cpr.2010.11.003

Mrazek, M. D., Franklin, M. S., Phillips, D. T., Baird, B., & Schooler, J. W. (2013). Mindfulness training improves working memory capacity and GRE performance while reducing mind wandering. Psychological Science, 24(5), 776-781.
https://doi.org/10.1177/0956797612459659

Zeidan, F., Johnson, S. K., Diamond, B. J., David, Z., & Goolkasian, P. (2010). Mindfulness meditation improves cognition: Evidence of brief mental training. Consciousness and Cognition, 19(2), 597-605.
https://doi.org/10.1016/j.concog.2010.03.014

TRY IT

The luxurious slow

Choose a tasty morsel. Place it in front of you.
Let your eyes take in its shape, colour, size.
Allow your nose to reach for its scent, your mouth to hanker for its taste on your tongue.
It's just you and the morsel.

No thoughts. No words.

You're ready.
Pick it up.
Feel its weight, its texture.

Take your First Bite.

Savour the taste, the texture,
the smell – slowly, deliberately.
Just you and the morsel.
Alone. Together.
Take your time. Swallow and wait.

Repeat.

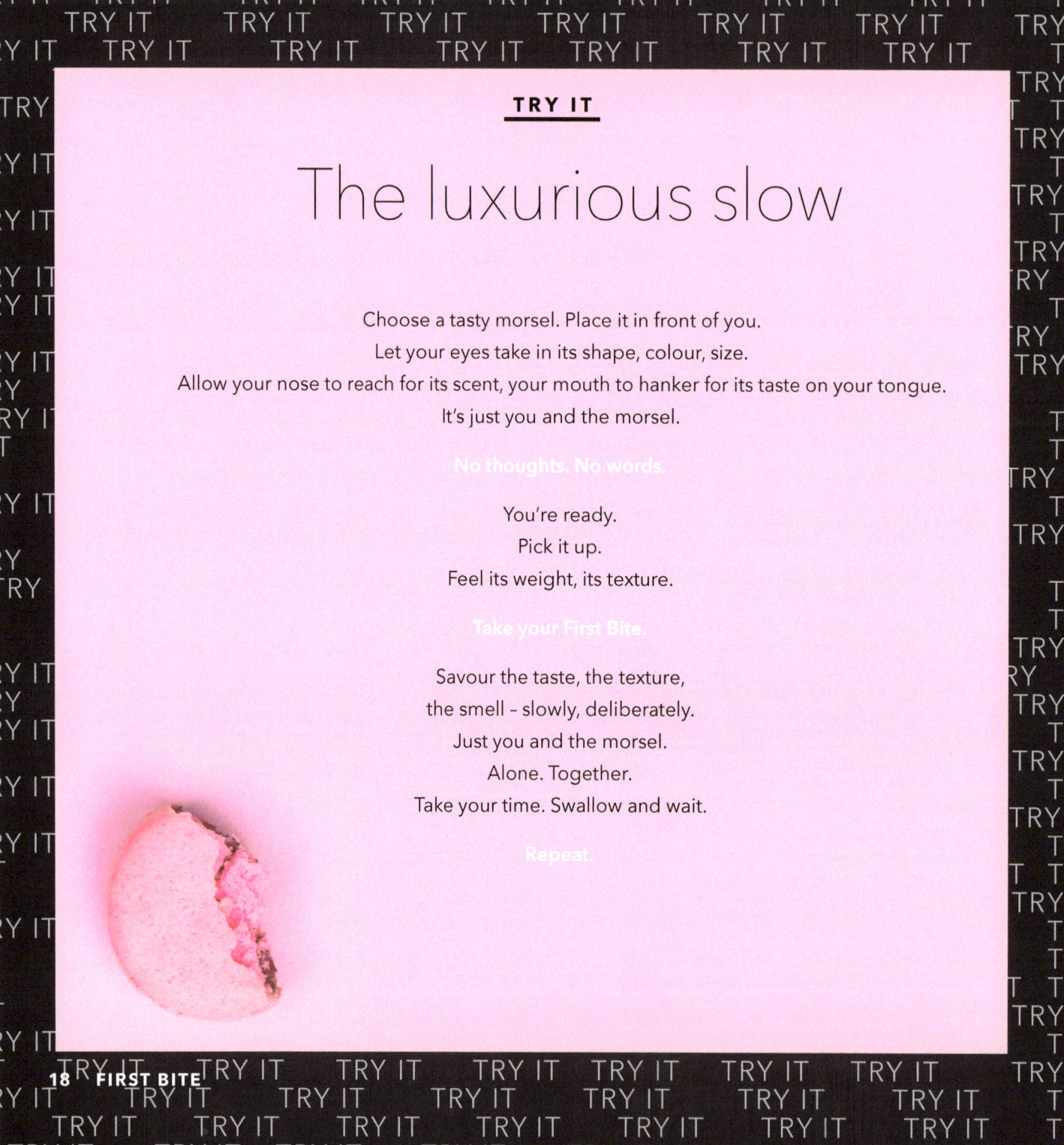

My big stop

I tried the *Luxurious slow*. Here's my experience.

My eyes meander over the nana-pink macaron. Hello my new friend, you look fine today. Picking it up, I'm a little distracted – thoughts are flipping between wanting to write this page as simply and honestly as I can, and that I'll be a total failure.

I let this thinking drop. Perhaps you will hear your own commentary, too: "This is silly." "There is no point to this." "What if someone is watching me." The objections are many but also they can be quite predictable. A bell curve would show that the most common thoughts are about being judged for being different or "out-grouped". The responses can also be quite predictable – often "screw them" or "fit in" arise.

Back to the macaron. I pause for a moment and let the thoughts drop away. Soon I feel quieter. Moments *seem* longer* – they're not really, but it feels that way. I feel sensitised.

I take the first bite. As I chew my macaron – I give my attention to it as much as possible. I don't describe anything. I don't try to identify ingredients. I don't say "sweet", "too sweet", "not sweet enough". And I don't channel Austin Powers and think "taste's kind of nutty". I definitely don't do that.

I'm just present, experiencing the food.

I'll be quiet now.
I'm going to take my second bite.

Confession

I had intended to try this yesterday – but can you believe, I still fell into autopilot. I completely forgot the First Bite. So if you forget too, don't feel bad – it will happen many times again, but stick with it because each time is worth it!

*Scientific studies suggest that the "stretching of time" in near death experiences is an evolutionary perception response. Time doesn't stretch but the information processed during those moments is far greater for the purposes of never repeating that situation again!
Ref: Graves, Lee. "Altered States. Scientists analyze the near-death experience". The University of Virginia Magazine, Summer 2007.

Chow down

Back in the '80s, I was lucky to score a job as an electronics technician at an early innovative computer company. I was green, straight out of university, and there was no staff induction, no training nor welcome to the company. I was simply plonked into a seat and introduced to Daryl. He eyed me with more than a hint of scepticism, it wasn't disdain but betrayed a clue that I'd be sweating it to earn his approval.

"Greeeeetings" – a laconic drawl that stretched long enough to make me squirm under his gaze. The smile indicated he liked tormenting small animals like me but it was just his way of play. No malice.

Daryl's eyes were cloudy with a pinkish tinge of spidery blood vessels in the sclera. I'd smoked a few joints in my time, so the tell-tale colour might be attributed to a pre-work bong and a Visine malfunction – but the cloudiness intimated health issues were at work.

Alvin, the boss, was a walking ice-breaker: jolly and upbeat, his approach was always foreshadowed by a nervous tic that was both physical and auditory. Daryl's drawl and Alvin's tic would make an excellent beat poet act or a boom-box rap. On this first morning, Alvin issued a staccato volley of jobs for Daryl to mentor me through.

He immediately called me "DJ" which was perceptive; less fortunately his Malaysian pronunciation of "Dazza" (for Daryl) sounded like "Daisy".

Daryl chirped, "Will do, Boss". It's hard to convey the likability of his demeanor, it was orthogonal to "cheerful" but if you remember Bugs Bunny characters, he was "Spike the Bulldog" and I was the earnest "Chester the Terrier".

Daryl was an Aussie – in that old school way. A biker and a geek, for him eating was not an art-form, it was a conquest. Hamburgers, chips and coke (I confess to loving two of that trinity). Daryl's entire hydration consisted of two-litre bottles of that fizzy pop.

Daryl's daily dietary secret was something I'd only seen occasionally before, during my childhood. He would chug – yep "scull" – an antacid called Mylanta. The website declares: "Fast relief from indigestion, heartburn, upset stomach, flatulence and wind pain".

With Daryl, there was a lot of gas: top and tail – and Mylanta was the go-to solution for this boy. One daily vignette was:
"Did you fart?"
"No"
"Must have been me then."

Jokes like that never get old. But Daryl's eyes, ruddy, dimpled skin and BMI portrayed a man in his 40s...he had just turned 30.

Wind forward a few decades. Mylanta materialised on my shopping list – two Nepalese superbug dysenteries in my 20s (left undiagnosed at the time) and 15 years of startup-founder stress had bequeathed me indigestion and an inflamed throat, so bad that coughing fits or loss of voice happened in sales meetings after an hour or so.

In a moment of insane despair, a visit to the GP set me on a path of specialists, voice coaches, nasal endoscopy (gotta love those) and a prescription for the long term use of Nexium.

Screw that.

A little research on Nexium reveals long-term use is not pretty. Instead my naturopath friend set me on a path to heal with apple cider vinegar, enzymes, concoctions of aloe vera and slippery elm.

But most importantly, two pieces of advice:

Firstly, breathe deeply into the belly before eating. This mindful preparation apparently switches on enzymes in the stomach to aid digestion. Secondly, chew.

If we eat while working, walking, driving or watching TV, then, for many of us, chewing and swallowing become completely unconscious and rushed. Biologically, chewing increases the surface area for your saliva's digestive enzymes to break the food down and prepare it for digestion.

If eating is a conquest for you (like me), swallowing too soon is loading up the stomach to do extra work and can lead to indigestion, inflammation and worse.

I wonder how Daryl's gut is faring? I'm sure there is farting.

THE SCIENCE

Saliva

Do you ever remember someone telling you why you should chew forty times?
What was **that** all about?

The benefits of saliva.

The Science™ tells us the mechanical process of chewing produces saliva which:

- introduces digestive enzymes like amylase and lipase
- has growth factors, like epidermal growth factor (EGF), which can promote wound healing. In some cultures, people lick their wounds as an instinctive response, which may provide a mild protective effect
- has antimicrobial agents, such as lysozyme, lactoferrin, and immunoglobulin A, that help protect against infection
- helps to neutralise the acids in the mouth, wash away food particles, and prevent the build-up of plaque.

Thus, creates a healthy oral environment.

The benefits of chewing as an exercise.

- The act of chewing strengthens the jaw muscles and promotes healthy teeth and gums.
- Chewing gives well-developed facial muscles contributing to a more defined jawline and facial structure – and outrageous good looks.
- For children and teens, the facial bones are still growing and developing, so chewing is essential.
- Do you grit or grind your teeth? Maybe this exercise will reduce that.

One Saturday at morning tea, I was scarfing down my cake and coffee all the time chatting. As I inhaled my cake, an older, more chill dude named Henryk joined me on the bench. With a playful smirk, Henryk said, "Young David" – he always called me that – "you might wanna slow down and chew your food more. I used to be a speed-eater like you, but trust me, chewing each bite about 40 times makes a difference."

Caught out, slightly embarrassed, I swallowed my pride (without chewing), yet intrigued by his unexpected advice, fired back "Why should I bother?" Henryk leaned back and drawled, "Enzymes… they need time to do their thing… breaking down the food and pulling out more nutrients. When I was a labourer, we ate a lot of crap: burgers, Chiko rolls, chips. I used to have some gnarly stomach issues, but once I started chewing more, things got way better."

With a grin, Henryk added, "Plus it keeps me trim, taut and terrific, chewing more means my brain gets the message that I'm full before I overdo it." For his age, Henryk did look fit and decades later, he still does.

So, forty chews – hard to do, but worth the effort.

Ron's napkin

He stood as I joined him. His old-fashioned manners and calm demeanour a marked contrast to the busyness of the city cafe. We sat. His active stillness, his aliveness, held me quiet, silent, not filling the space with the usual inane chit-chat.

Orders placed, he reached for the serviette holder – the metal box kind with small tissue-thin serviettes stacked within. Taking one in his hands, he began to unfold it, one fold at a time, opening it and flattening the crease to smooth it. Then the next fold, opened, and smoothed carefully in his fingers. Each fold, one after another, quiet in concentration, taking all the time he needed, separate from the rush all around.

I sat, watching, feeling his calm permeate me and our little space – as he finished, the serviette finally one flat surface. He reached over and handed it to me, then took another from the metal holder to begin the process again.

Our drinks arrived, steaming pots of English breakfast tea with tiny milk jugs and an old-fashioned, gold-rimmed plate bearing two small fruit tarts with glistening tops. Never had I felt less distracted by the noise and bustle surrounding us. We existed alone, in our own space, in our own quiet, pouring tea, holding our mini tarts over a carefully smoothed paper serviette, ready.

Morning tea

Everyone started to gather again. The day's activities on hold for the buffet morning tea. Trestle tables had been arranged end to end along the verandah and topped with bright floral cloths, plates and serviettes and an array of savoury and sweet treats. At the far end, tea and coffee were being served from large stainless-steel urns.

Clutching his plate in both hands, he eyed the table like a child at a birthday party. But this tall man, silver-haired, neatly dressed in a fine, pale blue sweater and jeans, was deep with wisdom. His eyes sparkled with delight at the choices, and his face showed that making a decision was almost impossible. His smile, the slightly mischievous demeanour, and the bursts of genuine joy that swept over his face instantly lifted the ordinariness that anyone around him might be feeling.

The choice was hard. The decision measured. But the joy remained evident as his hand moved decisively toward a freshly baked rock cake, sliced through and layered with a thin coating of butter.

Sitting on the garden bench, plate balanced on his knees, coffee cup next to him, he gazed as if looking inward, eyes half-closed, at his plate. With delicate fingers he lifted the rock cake to his mouth, taking his first bite. The rest he returned to his plate as he closed his eyes once again briefly, seeming to take in every flavour, every sensation, every texture.

He continued to savour the mouthful, eyes opened now, but still with an inward feel, taking in the group of people around him. They are scattered in groups and pairs on benches and seats, and even on rugs on the grass, chatting quietly or eating in silence.

He chats too, though every bite, every sip seems like his first – exquisite and unique to be fully experienced. Time loses meaning and stretches. I see myself sitting on the sandstone bench, tea in one hand and the moreish homemade biscuit in the other. A stillness separates me from the gathering, no thoughts, the sounds around me turned down. I take my first bite. I close my eyes. I take in the crisp biscuit, buttery and textured, hear the crunch, and feel the smooth, silky, lemony cream. They play in my mouth, a blissful combination. I open my eyes, ready for my next first bite.

He was my teacher. Through him, I learned to be still and aware that there is more. I miss him.

THE SCIENCE

Peeling back the onion

In *The luxurious slow* (*page 18*) you experienced simply the sensation of First Bite. Our spoiled society directly responds to the richness of experience by labelling things and making them ordinary. You may have found that the exquisite sensation that washed over you during First Bite had become numb by the time fifth or sixth bite was happening. You may have found you were back on autopilot and eating was just a transactional event again.

If you noticed this, that is awesome! This is metacognitive awareness in action, and you've already built some **muscle** for tapping in to more of this valuable faculty. As with mindful meditation, this small opening applied daily will become more available to you.

Much more likely is that the meal was finished and you didn't notice. This is because your **muscle** is small – it will grow with practice. This has repeated countless times for me, so don't feel like Robinson Crusoe – you are not alone. But it gets better.

Until now we have made the extraordinary into the very, very ordinary over time. You may have even heard the term "chasing the dragon" in the world of drugs, which describes how the neural pathways adapt to the drug, needing larger and larger doses to attain the same effect. So this process of making every recurring event ordinary has a strong biological and neurological basis that is locked into our evolutionary ascendancy. For eating, we want to reverse this mediocrity and let **presence** awaken us to the ecstatic dimensions that food offers.

Our brains are wired for novelty. Our **presence** in this moment, right now, makes the novelty.

For more on this:
BrainWorld Magazine - The Importance of Novelty, September 5, 2019 Nicole Dean
https://brainworldmagazine.com/the-importance-of-novelty/

TRY IT

Three mindful breaths

In a mindful state we can deepen our preparation and induce a relaxation response. This response engages the parasympathetic nervous system, responsible for restoring the body to a relaxed state after a stress response, calming it down, lowering the heart and respiratory rate, blood pressure and muscle tension. On page 22 we explained the digestive benefits.

This practice of taking three mindful breaths can help you to refresh, to be more present, to get off autopilot, to make a choice about what to do next.

TRY IT Take three breaths

First breath
Complete yet gentle attention to the process of breathing.

Second breath
Let the body relax.

Third breath
Ask, "What's most important now?"

WHEN TO DO THIS?

Before an important conversation.
When you feel triggered by something.
Before you transition from being at work to being home.
When you have the urge to check your phone or social media.

Thanks to SIYLI

Ma's madeira

I didn't know my grandmother very well. She died when I was still quite young. But the images I do have of her in my mind are crystal-clear and mostly pink! You see, she was a small woman, and wore no other colour but pink – in all its shades, from a deep rose skirt to the palest of shell pink silk bloomers. She had been a milliner in her younger years, and still kept a collection of beautiful hats she had made. Their home was in an old, dark-timber armoire in the spare bedroom.

Once a week my mother and I would walk to Ma's house for a visit. Her house was fancier than ours so I loved going, but it was quite a long walk for a small person. Once there, we would have afternoon tea out in the sunroom at the very long table that filled most of the space. Only one small end was set to accommodate us. And always there were the same two or three items of food on offer – Sao biscuits (that classic Aussie savoury square) with thinly sliced tomato (no butter), plain small round biscuits coated with chocolate, and slices of madeira cake. Now that I think about it, there was never anything homemade.

I loved the chocolate biscuits – such a treat as we almost never had those at home. Ma would always choose a slice of madeira cake. Taking her knife, she would cut the slice into nine squares, and eat one at a time, slowly and deliberately.

Ma

"It was hard living through the war and the Depression," my mother had said. Food was scarce and no doubt she would have made sure her three boys were fed properly before herself. Those memories don't really leave you. She never ate a lot, my mother recalled, but every bite was eaten slowly and savoured.

My mother laughed, thinking back about the squares of cake. "She was particular and so neat!" The beautiful image of her hats, more than a dozen neatly pinned to the padded sides or resting on stands in the spare room cupboard. There was no doubt in my mind that was where my father got his neat habits from.

These days, I wonder if she was a product of her past or just a mindful eater, many decades before it became a thing. And whenever I find myself with a slice of cake like that, I too cut it into nine squares, and eat each square slowly and deliberately, thinking of her.

Years later, when I was helping Mum sort through her old photos, we happened upon a very old black-and-white photo of Ma as a young woman, the only photo my mother had of her. She didn't look familiar to me at all. There is certainly none of the tiny delicate pinkness that I remember her by.

TRY IT

Origins

We live in a blessed time.

As you sit at the table, just glance at your phone that is sitting face up looking at you, ready to bleat out new alerts, messages and distractions. Note how it's so close to you.

Without touching it, ponder the complexity of the device and how many human hands and robots have been involved to construct this and transport it to you.

The battery alone is made of materials that come from many different countries. It is mined, refined and ingeniously machined into a form that is an encapsulated connection of leads and contact plates – processed into a tiny miracle.

It's the same for the billions of silicon junctions that implement unfathomably complex possibilities in just a few milliseconds. The screen and its protective glass and touch-sensitive coating all profoundly sophisticated and intricate in their invention and implementation.

So too with your food. Are you having smashed avo on sourdough today?
As you take your next meal, quietly reflect on the individual elements of it, where they were farmed, the farmers, their families, the truck drivers that transported the produce, the packaging that protected it.

If you want to go further, consider the food preparation implements: the knives, the frying pan, the toaster, the oven's manufacturing processes and materials.
Your plates and bowls…the list is endless.

Can you be grateful for all these people?
Take a moment. Rest your eyes on what is in front of you.
Breathe and follow its journey to you…
and maybe, turn your phone face-down.

TRY IT

Guided gratitude meditation

Prior to eating.

As you sit down to enjoy your meal, take a moment to pause and fully appreciate the food before you. Close your eyes and take a deep breath, allowing the aroma of the meal to gently awaken your senses.

Begin by acknowledging the source of your food. Connect with the earth from which it emerged, the soil that provided the nutrients for its growth, and the sun that warmed it and gave it life. Envision the vast fields or orchards, teeming with life, each plant carefully nurtured by the elements and the loving hands of those who tended to them.

Take a deep breath in, and as you exhale, allow yourself to feel gratitude for the sun, the soil and the water that played a crucial role in the growth of the food on your plate. Acknowledge the incredible life-supporting value of these elements that have come together to nourish your body and soul.

Breathe

As you breathe in, focus on the nutritional value of your meal. Each bite contains essential vitamins, minerals and nutrients that your body needs to thrive. Recognise the power of the food to heal, nourish, and energise your body as you take each mindful bite.

As you continue to breathe deeply, turn your focus to the energy that was used to bring this food to your table. Recognise that energy consumption is a necessary part of all life, but also that it can be conserved and used more mindfully. Allow this awareness to help you commit to making conscious choices in your daily life to reduce your own waste.

Accept

Finally, take a moment to embrace acceptance. Understand that your meal is the result of a complex and interconnected process. With this knowledge, let yourself feel gratitude for the opportunity to partake in this shared experience.

Inhale deeply, feeling the energy of the universe flow into your body, and as you exhale, let go of any remaining tension or unease. Open your eyes, and before you take your first bite, take a moment to truly appreciate the food before you.

First Bite

As you eat, continue to breathe deeply and mindfully, savouring each bite and remaining present in the experience. Allow yourself to fully absorb the nourishment and love that has been poured into your meal, knowing that it will support you in living a healthy, conscious, and energy-conserving life.

TRY IT

Partner meditation

First Bite for two.

Setting the stage

Taking First Bite to your family and friends can be socially awkward, so try starting with a close friend. This requires open communication, shared interest, empathy and patience.

Discuss or share this book with your friend, perhaps use the place cards or drink coasters as a way to "break the ice". Share your experiences, encourage them to share their experiences too – be curious; this promotes a safe space for growth. Fully engage in the moment. Understand that progress may be slow. Gradually, your attention will shift from the awkwardness to the present.

•

Let's step through it:
Find a comfortable position with your friend at the dinner table. Close your eyes and synchronise your breaths, inhaling and exhaling together, releasing tension, fully engaging in the moment. Together, focus on the ambient sounds, acknowledging their **presence** without judgment. Reopen your eyes and observe the food's colours and textures. Take in the aromas.

Take your first bite. As you taste, mindfully savour the flavour. During conversation, maintain focus on the present moment, the shared experience. If awkwardness arises, return your attention to the sensory experience, the taste of the food, your friend's voice, the sounds around you.

This isn't about perfection, but a shared practice and mindful **presence** at the dinner table. The key is constant practice and mutual support.

TRY IT

More place cards

_____
Connect with your food, from farm to fork

_____
Pause, breathe, and fully experience the joy of eating

_____
With gratitude, I appreciate this meal's source

_____
Channel your inner sloth: eat slowly, savour every bite, and live in the delicious moment

_____
Chew slowly, savour the flavours, and appreciate the moment

_____
Listen to your body's wisdom as you enjoy your meal

_____
Taste the love and care in every morsel

_____
Find delight in each bite, nourishing both body and soul

_____

Slow down, the food isn't going anywhere

_____

Fall in love with your food

_____

Take in all the colours and textures

_____

The wolf ain't at the door, don't wolf down your food

_____

Sit, slow down, savour, simplify, and smile

_____

Imagine you're a food critic – describe each bite to your imaginary fans!

> Printable templates can be found at
> firstbite.world

Drink coasters

Pause, breathe and
appreciate each sip

Drink in the moment,
savour the flavours

Sip with intention,
savour with gratitude

Printable templates can be found at
firstbite.world

Next steps... over to you

In the introduction, we suggested:

"First Bite is a simple call-to-action,

to start each and every meal with three mindful bites,

and observe the contribution to your life and others around you."

Such a task can be magical or mechanical.

If it feels like a burden then your energy in that moment is not ready.

Give yourself time to find the spark, the **aliveness**. It's only a breath away.

TRY IT yourself

TRY IT with a close friend

Take a chance and **TRY IT** with a group

good luck!

Image credits

Cover, **iv**, **v** Pamela Bray **vi** unsplash-wilhelm-gunkel **4, 7, 8** Pamela Bray **10** unsplash-sonnie-hiles
14 unsplash-thomas-evans **18** unsplash-keila-hotzel **20** pexels-daniel-reche **24** unsplash-ali-yahya
26 unsplash-melissa-walker-horn **30** unsplash-loverna-journey **32** Unknown-Bray family archive
33 unsplash-stock.adobe **35** unsplash-caroline-attwood **37** unsplash-frances-allarotti **39** unsplash-louis-hansel

www.ingramcontent.com/pod-product-compliance
Lightning Source LLC
Chambersburg PA
CBHW041159290426
44109CB00002B/69